CELINE'S SALON

THE ANTHOLOGY

~Volume 1~

Edited by
Lucy Tertia George

Cover artwork by Garry Salter
Proofread by Polly Bull

Wordville
www.wordville.net
info@wordville.net

INTRODUCTION

It all started with Gertrude Stein.

'You are extraordinary within your limits,' she once exclaimed, 'but your limits are extraordinary!'

Born in Paris, and always intrigued by the bohemian Parisian set, Celine took Stein's words and ran with them. Her love of French cabaret inspired what has become Celine's Salon, a 'literary cabaret' that features the best poetry, song writing, short stories and prose, and has been popping up on stages across London and internationally since 2016.

The mission of Celine's Salon is to create a platform that nurtures new and established artists and offers the audience an entertaining and enlightening experience. The audience at Celine's is loyal and warmly inviting. Nervous first-timers are encouraged to share their work and experienced performers get the chance to trial new material and experiment. Each event is unique.

Audience and performers together create a literary community that encourages creativity, championing the literary journey, from scrap of paper to published book. Performing to a live audience, with immediate feedback and support, inspires an artist to grow, enjoying freedom of expression in the bohemian sense and developing confidence in one's own voice.

The interplay of established writers and new writers allows genius in all its guises to flourish in a nurturing environment. Novices glean insights from published authors and accomplished professionals gain new inspiration. Literary foundlings are fostered and given a home. Networking abounds and, most importantly, the whole experience is fun.

Each salon has a chosen theme in which writers are encouraged to riff on a topic, opening up new avenues in their work. Whether it's *The Seven Deadly Sins* or *The Art of Laughter*, the theme gives performers the chance to stretch their repertoire. No idea is out of bounds or off limits. Something new is always possible.

Gathering at Celine's Salon means rubbing shoulders with experts in publishing or catching up with a charismatic raconteur. An early idea, that spark of inspiration scrawled on a beer mat, could one day become a best seller. Mentoring relationships formed at the salon have led to book and record deals, and many thousands of words of original content.

The friendships that have come out of the salon are invaluable. Everyone is welcome and treated equally, whether Booker Prize winner or hesitant, stammering newcomer. Snobbishness has no place and accessibility is a given. Celine's goal is to give everyone, whoever they are, a platform and a voice.

All are rewarded with the most entertaining of hosts. Singing *The Lady of Soho*, *The Tidal Basin* or *Lord Butterfly*, as she struts between tables and chairs to the delight of an entranced audience, Celine is true to the tradition of cabaret and music hall. Entertainment, grounded in raucous joie de vivre, is embodied by the host herself.

The heady combination of literature and performance in clamouring Soho, infused with a Parisian sensibility, is a one off.

This anthology can't possibly hope to recreate the atmosphere of the quirky, high-energy evenings we've spent together at Celine's Salon. But we have collected work from some of the 'regulars' for your enjoyment. We couldn't fit everyone in—there's already talk of a Volume 2—but we hope that this anthology gives you a flavour of the wide range of creativity that is drawn together through Celine's Salon. We may be limited by page number and word count, but even within these paraments, we hope Gertrude would agree the results are extraordinary.

Wordville

———◆◆◆———

ABOUT CELINE HISPICHE

Celine is a London-based writer and performer with a monthly show on Soho Radio that celebrates diverse writing and performance. She spent three years in New York, performing stand-up comedy, returning to the UK to develop a variety of musicals and productions, performing at events and festivals around the country and across the world.

Thanks to all the writers, poets, singers, artists, comedians, storytellers, magicians, raconteurs and musicians who have performed at Celine's Salon:

Olivier F. Adam, Andry Anastasis-McFarlane, **Steven Appleby**, **Barney Ashton-Bullock**, Zata Banks, Lady Sandra Bates, Alexa Bauer, **Maria Beadell**, Mickey Beans, Kim Benson, Isabella Bornholt, Takeru Brady, Buster Bray, Louis Brennan, Marie Brenneis, Andrea Britton, **Andrew Brown**, Camilla K. Bryant, **Polly Bull**, Nick Butt, Aidan Casserly, **Ashley Chapman**, **Ryan Child**, Megan Choritz, Stephen Coates, Darren Coffield, Colossal H & Da Stigma, William Corbett, Nick Cox, Dave Crocker, Dennis Da Silva, **Jo Danzig**, Jo D'arc, Clancy Gebler Davies, Sasha De Suinn, Matt Devereaux, Steve Devereaux, Zoe Devlin, Raphael D'Lugoff, **Rachel Dreyer**, Paul Duane, Gary Dunnington, Don Eales, Lynzey Eddy, EST, Steven EvEns, Gary Fairfull, Claire Felstead, Vanessa Helen Fenton, **Cathy Flower**, Shannyn Fourie, Dennis Francis, Matt Francomb, Geraint Friswell, G3, Lynne Gentle, Jenna Gleespen, Salena Godden, Romani Graham, **Tony Green**, Andrew Greenfield, Michael Groce, **Gis Harris**, **Matt Harvey**, Maurice Hatt, Maria Heath Beckett, **Celine Hispiche**, Annette Holzwarth, Christopher Howell, Madeleine Kate Hyland, Mikkel Juel Iversen, Philippe Jakko, Sarah Janes, **Amina Jindani**, Godfrey, Johnson, Naomi Jones, Marika Josef, Matt Joy, Jonathan Kemp, Thoby Kennet, Alex Klineberg, George Landee, **Clayton Littlewood**, Samantha Love, Anna Lucas,

Lunatics Lost, **Seki Lynch**, **Lucy Lyrical**, Lewis Macleod, Jaelith Mahoney, Simon Matthews, Jenny Matthias, **Thomas McColl**, Dave McGowan, Bentley Bizzibee Moore, Gabriel Moreno, **Heather Moulson**, Robin Munro Runciman, **NaMo**, Claire Nicholson, Kate Normington, Golnoosh Nour, Jamila Omar, **One Voice, One Cello & a Mad Belgian**, Jane Palm-Gold, John Pearse, Misha Pimington, Pinkie, Anna Pool, Robert Pugent, Rev D. Wayne Love, **Zelda Rhiando**, Iain Richards, Red Richardson, James Richmond, Emma Rose, Paul Ryan, Sigrún Sævaradóttir-Griffiths, **Sasha & The Shades**, Garry Salter, Tom Salter, Oliver Sam, Benjamin Savage, Derek Savage, Sidney Scallan, **Santa Semeli**, Ibrahim-Farouk Sesay, Garry Sharp, Mieko Shimizu, George Simmonds, Kae Skinner, Kevin Skinner, Clifford Slapper, Lilly Slaptsilli, Mila Smith, Soho Radio, Philip Spalding, Amey St. Cyr, Laura Stark, Sarah Stockbridge, Adonis Storr, Chris Sullivan, Maggie Swampwino, The Handlers, The Messengers, The Slaughtered Lambs, Erika Thornley, Trowse Tommaso, Arturo Edoardo, Tiffany Anne Tondut, Tenpole Tudor, **Tom Turner**, Colin Vaines, Mark Wallinger, Carissa Warner, Dai Watts, Christine Weir, Scarlet West, Alexander Wild, **Rebecca Anne Willis**, **Douglas Graham Wilson**, Tim Woodward, Jatta Young, **Louisa Young** and Wendy Young.

CONTENTS

Part One

Part Two

Part Three

Part Four

INTERVAL

Part Five

Part Six

Part Seven

CURTAIN

PART ONE

Celine Hispiche
Barney Ashton-Bullock
Amina Jindani
Matt Harvey

CELINE HISPICHE

A LADY OF SOHO

When in Bloomsbury you must have met
The divine Doomsbury Set
You'll see them from far away
They do put on a display

Large feathers in hats
Black and white spats
Oh, colourful tweeds
Hands covered in beads
Laughing and joking
Pipes they are smoking
They are the Doomsbury Set

When walking the streets of Fitzrovia
Donning a suit from a tailor
Fresh off the boat from Dover
A drunken falling French sailor
And propping up the bar
A woman who's lost her teeth
It's good to keep afar
She's known as the toothless thief
We are the Doomsbury Set!

When walking the streets of Soho
In the steps of bohemian ghosts
There's something we all should know
We now play their hosts
And lent up against a street light
She'll tell you never to go
A very familiar sight
A lady of Soho!

I'm a lady, don't you know?
In the shadow of Soho
A woman of demure
A familiar character
Never getting too demonic
Whilst sipping gin and tonic
I'm a lady, don't you know?
A lady of Soho

I love to take a stroll
To the nearest watering hole
Another face in the transient crowd
Feel the warmth of my decadent shroud
Male friends purely platonic
Talking business, how ironic!
I'm a lady, don't you know?
A lady of soho

Neon signs and flashing lights
Drunk girls and laddered tights
A sea of sex and sleaze
Where hustlers take and tease
Sweet nothings in many ears
The laughter and the tears
I'm a wanderer, don't you know?
The old streets of Soho
The artists and the dreamers
The beggars and road sweepers
The tickets and the touts
The laughter and the shouts
I'm a lady, don't you know?
A lady, don't you know?
A lady of ... a lady of ... a lady of Soho!

———————◗ ◆ ◆ ◗———————

This song was performed at Celine's Salon on 12 Feb 2016 at The Society Club.

BARNEY ASHTON-BULLOCK

YET, JUST A BLURRY INSTAMATIC . . .

Just a blurry Instamatic of a beautiful oblivion;
your pulse of molten honeyed cuss splurged
amphet emphatic 'cross empathies so tautly gut
strung; aggressive passivities 'midst the berserk
crosswinds of all our jading, estranging, ageing lives.

Yeh! We who'd meanly thrived a while
decrying those who'd run 'empty to depot'
or into sand-drags and cul-de-sacs headlong,
when we were wired and unreasoned,
when we were high and couldn't know
that for every passing night train seen,
there'd be many that ran slow
and yet still made their way to Jesus
on some hallowed old railroad.

Uninvited revenants
can sabotage their deities.
Ad hoc flash-mob choirs gnarl
their by-rote chew of your psalmic 'Hallelujah' as a
latterday laical 'Amazing Grace'
in a virtue-signalled, idolatrous, paean deadpan.
(With a side order of triple fried tears sigh-cried, m'dead dear!)

Their churn of appropriated 'Hosannas' amaze me.
Their strewn, flung flumes of approximated levities
that bomb-rush bang the tenderer quietudes of resolve.
It is such, we meek and merciful fans are slain whilst
in smulchy meditative mood; our mourn allayed.

As a grazed petal in a wind buffed descent might
skitter its chapped whispers until its end around
the remnants of diminished sonant range, and
gruffer mauls of declarations made, so,
luscious lowing Cohen intoned, stentorian steady,
ethereal as an icicles last twist of gliss,
his proffered profundities, so profoundly missed
and, yet, by most ignored as we, forlorn
satellites, drift half-kiss to half-kiss within
the interstice of the self-same gyres of
the 'sacred' and 'profane', yet, tardily realise they
said of Madame Thatcher too, 'We will not know
their like again'...

Just a blurry Instamatic of a beautiful oblivion;
we remnant cones of desiccant, we debris of
disciples who burnt, with you, in you, for you,
in the immanent umbra and in the protective Arc
of your sainted, yet secular, book of sensu-songs
that frond our hubris, our hubris frond.

L'ANTI-ARRIVISTE EST PARTI

Even within the abhorrence of absence
is a marked aberrance of pulsing joy
we are left conveyancing the wounds
we are abeyant to their melodic seep
your intuit repertoire of counter-hex
your quasi-bittersweet loll of lyrical intrigue—

Here, a sallow heart inflates with hope
there, a hollow mind tolls in outreach
we are all but trough-laden, sod-bound arrivistes
cusping it, winging it, drowning in it someday
therein be the tragedy, the mystery, the mirth
the orientation is the destination—

For when, to a sailor, the sea is as mildew in motion
its wonderment worn to slicken sick liqueform veldts
its waves puckering in indigest, vomiting for revolution
for when, to that sailor, the ambics of trussing waves
testify in their throt of malaise; their unchewed tether
of gruelly variegations lap 'round slung, trash-forms a-ripple—

Pollutant detritus, deleterious of such seafarers' safety
sizes serried from swirling particulate to the lumpen, sunken
dumped 'white goods' sea-bed bedrocks of corrosive causticities
we, shoreline blind to this immersed bind of junk cluster
ever await for a hallowed sunset, imbuing it with miracle
with the cure, the penance, the forgiveness; a prophecy—

Just as you soothsay sang it, mister
residuous and resonant
in shalom and amen.

———————➤ ◆ ◆ ◆ ◀———————

These poems were performed at Celine's Salon *Obsession* on 13 May 2019 at
Gerry's Club. Both appeared in *Avalanches in Poetry*. Barney has three books of
poetry published: *Café Kaput!* (Broken Sleep Books), *F**kpig Zeitgeist!* and
Bucolicism (Cherry Red Records). He is the songwriter/lyricist in the 'Andy Bell
is Torsten' band and the poet/narrator of the Downes Braide Association.

AMINA JINDANI
WAU BULAN

A

Wau

Soaring

Skywards,

Shaping shadows in the sunset hues, like souls on strings.

The paddy field's tropical textures—a tapestry of folded husks heaving

In the breeze and breaking into rugged rustling sounds, whispering

Against the soft singing musical notes of dusk. Yet, the wau harmonises

A wistful tune of tomorrow's dreams with the gentle humming of a

Lullaby; an eternal empathetic encounter with evening's promise that,

Beyond sleep, another day starts and sets like this one.

A wau

In

The

Wind

Hushes

Heartbeats

Into the new folding of

Night and creates the sacred spaces in time.

But, just like the crescent moon-shaped tail, the wau promises

Another new dawn to begin again. But does the new generation, who

Share their forefathers' passion for the soul-souring heights for their

Own hopes and dreams, see the poetic lull of flying the ancient wau

And laying down to catch its song?

Do they know how the moon

Waxes and wanes to the winnowing

Windborne wau?

Do

They

See

How?

———————■ ◆ ◆ ■———————

This poem was performed at Celine's Salon YouTube show on 8th April 2021.
Amina is a drama educator from Wimbledon now residing in Malaysia.
A wau bulan is an intricately designed Malaysian moon-kite.

7

MATT HARVEY
SAY IT WITH FLOWERS – A TIME-LAPSE LOVE STORY

From his garden he could see her garden, as she his, from hers. He realised she was the woman from the garden centre. She'd smiled at him. He'd smiled back. He saw her hastily putting down *Pride and Prejudice* when he came to buy his things. She'd blushed.

He went back three days running, bought things he needed in small batches, then things he didn't need in smaller batches. 'Thank you.'

He earned 500 loyalty points, and they gave him a string bag of bulbs. Which gave him an idea.

He chose a patch and planted them. 'YOUR BEAUTIFUL'. No apostrophe. No e. They didn't all come up.

YO   BE   IF

He wondered if she'd got the message. Or any message. Probably not. Time passed.

Come Spring, after the first snowdrops, there, in neat crocuses: 'PARDON?'

Surging with adrenalin he bought two bags of bulbs. All the same this time. Fritillaries. Tenderly reiterated: 'U R BEAUTIFUL'.

There, he'd said it. The wait was difficult. Then they didn't really synchronise. While some were still just peeking through the soil the keen ones spelt: UTIFU. The rest would catch up soon. Before they did though, strong winds in the night flattened the UTI.

She woke to the message: F U

He panicked. He should have fluffed up the others, propped them with sticks if necessary, instead he mowed them all down, hoped she'd not seen.

Puzzled, but enjoying the botanical banter, she planted blue, yellow and red primula: F U 2.

He was crestfallen. Would not trust fritillaries ever again. Painstakingly he planted penitent red lupins. OOPS SORRY. Then across his former lawn with cornflowers, NO OFFENCE MEANT

Feeling for him, she replied in January, NONE TAKEN—in snowdrops planted compassionately but perhaps not as carefully as before. What he saw was: I M TAKEN

A bitter blow. He knew what he had to do. Bravely he planted hardy pansies, let his house and rented a flat.

She was sorry to see him go, and surprised to read GOODBYE, GOOD LUCK.

Two years later he moved back. She spotted him, out tidying the garden the tenant had let slide.

Shyly she planted grape hyacinth. HI. He responded cautiously, in delphiniums, HI. She, in careful crocuses: R U OK?

He'd had enough. Speak and be damned. He blurted out, in unequivocal red tulips bought full-grown. 'I ♡ U'

She replied almost immediately, a smiley face in happy marigolds.

Marigolds. Marry-golds. Yes. He began to dig, his trench so deep she could read 'WILL YOU...' She went indoors to sow seeds in a tray.

Before his bulbs came up she was knocking on his door, tea-tray in hands, her eyes inviting him to pull back the covering tea-towel. Revealed, in stenciled cress, the word, YES.

———◆◆◆———

This story was performed at Celine's Salon *The Art of Laughter* at The Barrel House Ballroom, Totnes on 13th October 2017.

Matt's way with words has taken him from Totnes to the Wimbledon Tennis Championships via Saturday Live, the Edinburgh Festival and the Work section of the Guardian. He is host of Radio 4's Wondermentalist Cabaret, creator of *Empath Man*, and author of *The Hole in the Sum of My Parts*, *Where Earwigs Dare*, *Mindless Body Spineless Mind* and, with artist Claudia Schmid, *Sit!* and *Careless Whisker.*

PART TWO

Lucy Lyrical
Heather Moulson
Tony Green
Maria Beadell

LUCY LYRICAL

TO BE FRANK

(Sung to the tune of *Crazy* by Willie Nelson)

Crazy, they say I'm an abomination.
Scary, a monster who's up to no good.
It's lonely, lonely up here on this mountain.
I know I'm misshapen—but I'm also misunderstood.

> Never, never judge this book by its cover.
> You know nothing till you've walked in another man's feet.
> I wish you'd take my second-hand hand, and
> Tell me I'm frightful but also delightful,
> And you're feeling crazy too.

I know it coz I've got the mind of a poet;
A poet dug up in the dark, à la carte.
It's stranger to look through the eyes of a stranger.
Surely, you see that I'm more than the sum of my parts?

> Never, never judge this book by its cover.
> You know nothing till you've walked in another man's feet.
> I wish you'd take my second-hand hand, and
> Tell me I'm frightful but also delightful,
> And you're feeling crazy too.

———◆◆◆———

This song was performed at Celine's Salon *Horror* on 6 July 2016 at The Society Club, with apologies to Willie Nelson, Patsy Cline and Mary Wollstonecraft Shelley.

Lucy Lyrical is also known as Lucy Tertia George, author of *Three Women*, published by Starhaven Press in 2018.

HEATHER MOULSON

LIFE ON MARS

I was sitting in class when I heard
He'd got to number three in the charts.
Mr George talked to us about English comprehension which I couldn't
remotely comprehend because that song was going round and round
in my head!

My friend says it's 'Sailors fighting in the dance hall....'
She's going out with a sixth former, so she knows everything!
Cockney Rebel this, Dory Previn that....
Who does she think she is?!
Lurking around the sixth form common room while I slink off home
miserably to listen to David Essex.

I don't like Bowie's LP
But I pretend I do to impress the sixth former's mates.
But then I have a snog with one of them,
I whispered huskily in his ear;
'I think Hunky Dory is shit!'
I ended up at the bus stop alone—
but victory was mine—I think.

———— • • • ————

This poem was performed at Celine's Salon YouTube show *Is There Life on Mars?* on 8th April 2021.

THE QUEUE

Look at these men ordering soya lattes!
Getting iPhones out to pay!
What is the world coming to?!

Why don't they have a strong cup of tea
with three sugars?! Like a real man!
And carry a wad of notes like me Dad.
And those bulging rucksacks, whatever
do they put in those things?!
Macs tied around their waist—
What do they look like?!

I'd like to see the manager of this establishment, please.
She was a friend of mine once.
Sexted night and day, sending
graphic pictures of herself to her latest fuck buddy.
Was romance completely dead?
I used to tell her; write him a love letter!
The dried saliva on the back of an envelope
more erotically charged than any vaginal close-up.

Oh yes! I'll have one of those buckets of coffee, please.
How much?! I'll have to do contactless!

——————◆ ◆ ◆ ———————

This poem was performed at Celine's Salon *Celebration of Berwick Street
Market* on 11 September 2017 at the Med Café, London.

14

COLOURS OF '73

Liz's wobbly thighs are purple with cold.
Limited heating, looming blackouts,
Everyone's seeing red.

My true-blue mum calls Heath a traitor.
What a dim view to take!
Speaking of which,
Liz says she's asked Paul Watkins round.
I go pink.

He says there's a new Slade Christmas song.
We put on Top of the Pops.
On the black and white screen, we can clearly see the colour of Noddy
Holder's trousers.

Paul, despite his worldliness,
Confesses that he'd never been to a party before.
He got off with Susan Turner.
He doesn't know whether to ask her out.
Despite kissing her for hours
To Python Lee Jackson,
She still doesn't set him on fire.

What was the point of all that smooching and snogging, if it's not going
to come to anything?!

And I wonder what colour Susan's love bites are today.
I know my face is turning green!
We give Slade a lukewarm reception,
That record will never catch on.

———————— ♦♦♦ ————————

This poem was performed at Celine's Salon *Vinyl* on 5 December 2016 at The
Society Club, London.

Heather has been performing extensively since 2017 in London and Surrey.
Her nostalgic pamphlet *Bunty, I Miss You* was published in 2019.

TONY GREEN

'WHO'S A SHAPE-SHIFTING LIZARD, THEN?'

'Look, I'm telling you they are!' exclaimed the large man wearing the mouse-coloured vicuña Fedora, and not for the first time. His voice betokened his size and just about every customer (it being Friday night there was more than usual) in the antiquated village inn must have heard him—with the possible exception of old Godfrey who was as deaf as that proverbial post.

The speaker was Denzil Stanhope-Fitzhardinge—a relative newcomer to the picture postcard town of Little Gidworth and now by far its number one conspiracy theorist.

'Even Graham the Greengrocer—and as we all know he wasn't exactly at the front of the queue when the brains were given out—told me only yesterday and I quote verbatim: 'They nutted Diana off cos' she fahnt aht abaht 'em and she went an' opened 'er gob din't she?''

Dr Sebastian Cringeworthy, the local medical practitioner, he of the dicky heart, had had just about enough and was yet again at the end of his tether. Before the arrival of Stanhope-Fitzhardinge, it was he who'd always held court at this pub table and had done so for a good twenty years; now he was lucky if he could get a word in.

'Oh, do shut up, Denzil. None of us—well, most of us anyway—are not in the least interested in hearing about your absurd and totally unfounded theories.'

The remark was ignored. 'Look at them: The Queen, Prince Phillip, the Queen Mother to take just three; most people don't live to be that old, do they?'

Once D.S.F. got going it was unlikely that a ten-ton truck could stop him. Cringeworthy left the assembly deciding that a little chat with the lascivious and oft odiferous Eton-educated barman Eric about the merits of Stinkowski's controversial Second Symphony would be a preferable alternative. It was even more galling that young William Blezard who'd only just graduated from St. John's, Cambridge with a double first, seemed to find D.S.F. so fascinating.

At his surgery the next day, Dr Cringeworthy felt a little under the weather—but he'd never been a slacker. He was, after all, getting on a bit and his heart was not in the best condition. He'd had to cut out his beloved fatty foods some years ago. Oh, for an egg and bacon sandwich. These days it was a macrobiotic diet. He popped his full-strength Atorvastatin tablet before seeing his first patient of the day, who turned out to be a new one, a chap called Denzil Stanhope-Fitzhardinge, would you believe it?

'Just what he needed,' he didn't think. D.S.F. was requiring a blood test. He noted that he and his new patient were of a similar age.

'Sebastian, my dear fellow!' he boomed. 'Good to see you after so long,' he joked. 'You know you really SHOULD take my theories much more seriously.' This he said with a, curious for him, cold precision.

Ignoring the remark which he saw as fatuous, Cringeworthy preceded to his business. 'A blood test, yes Mr Stanhope-Fitzhardinge ... yes, a man of your age ... our age, should have such tests on a regular basis.'

There was a huge knowing Cheshire cat smile spread across D.S.F.'s large face. What came out of the vein in his arm was not a deep red colour but a luminescent GREEN!

'What?'

'I told you, didn't I? About shape-shifting lizards but you, the determined rationalist, refused to believe. Now you know the truth. You could even find it in my assumed name if you'd looked.'

At that moment, Cringeworthy, who could no longer doubt, found himself looking at just such a creature and it was far more hideous than he could ever have dreamed of. The shock was simply too much. Nevertheless, it was a quick and relatively painless death. Resuming his human form again D.S.F. put the syringe in his pocket and informed the receptionist that the doctor had had a heart attack.

Young William Blezard took over the Surgery shortly afterwards.

This story was performed at Celine's Salon *The Supernatural* on 28 March 2018 at Hummus Bros, London. Tony has worked as an actor and a stand-up comedian (arguably a 'verbalist').

MARIA BEADELL

TILIKUM

Dedicated to the 60 wild-caught orcas still in captivity.

Stolen from my home in the Icelandic seas
The waves echoing my mother's desperate pleas
Wrenched from the bosom of my tribe
The fear I felt, I cannot describe

Crammed into an aquatic cage
I was bullied by strangers from an early age
Then forced to perform for tourists who clapped and cheered
Every time this humiliated creature appeared

Floating listlessly in my gaol
This is no place for a whale
My majestic fins flaccid from confinement
My body deformed and out of alignment

But most of all my mind, increasingly unsound
As I obey my human masters
In this lunatic compound

Until one day I can take it no more
My good-natured trainer that I adore
Becomes the victim of my pent-up rage
When I momentarily break out of my cage
And end her life with one swift motion
Remembering my birth right as a predator of the ocean

And I kill again and again and again,
But they continue to keep me in my pen
Flipping my fins and waving to the crowd
Like a wind-up toy
I hope they're proud

I even got on the news
'Finally, they'll understand what it's like in my shoes!'
I thought... but I was wrong
'A tragic trick that just went wrong'
'The killer whale went mad,' they said, then the story was put to bed.

And back I went, back to my concrete gaol
Crammed in with others, too small for a whale
My cries for help falling on deaf ears
The chlorine in this aquarium burns away my tears
And so the show goes on, just as before
Another leap, another flip, the people want more!
Until finally it's time for my ultimate trick,
The one where I get fatally sick.

Banished, I am left to die alone,
Well before my time, no tribe to call my own
And after some time, as I gasp my last breath,
I say goodbye to my tiny tank of death.

And so, it ends, and I am gone
The psycho beast, once so strong
Is but a distant memory
Broken spirit released and, finally, free.

———————— ♦ ♦ ♦ ————————

This poem was performed at Celine's Salon on 8th April 2021 on Soho Radio, London.

SPORADIC LOVE - AN ODE TO THE AVOIDANT LOVER

A sensual touch / a pat on the back
Sporadic love ... what I'm used to.

A peck on the forehead / a disgusted look
Sporadic love ... what I'm used to.

A lingering glance / a cold shoulder
Sporadic love ... what I'm used to.

A cute nickname / a brutal put down
Sporadic love ... what I'm used to.

A call everyday / radio silence
Sporadic love ... what I'm used to.

An unexpected visit /a last minute let down
Sporadic love ... what I'm used to.

A handmade gift / a dagger through the heart
Sporadic love ... what I'm used to.

A shuddering orgasm / a yawning emptiness
Sporadic love ... what I'm used to.

A smouldering stare / a dismissive look
Sporadic love ... what I'm used to.

One glad eye for me / and always one for her
Sporadic love ... what I'm used to.

———————◆◆◆———————

This poem was performed at Celine's Salon *Brief Encounters* on 25 March 2019 at Gerry's Club, London.

Maria Beadell is a writer, painter and performer dabbling in the world of comedy, music and cabaret. As 'Mariainpaint' she creates fantasy and surrealist art.

PART THREE

Polly Bull
Sasha & The Shades
Zelda Rhiando
Douglas Graham Wilson

POLLY BULL

KINGS CROSS 2.0

Spit with strength at the shape-shift station.
We are wiping away muck with no placation.
Sweep, sweep, sweep the imperfects away.
There is a gold-tied man with his gold-drenched display.

Set fire to the dustbins, set fire to the bedraggled.
Kick the stench up the road where the marketeers haggled.
Close your eyes to the death storm, don't look left or right.
We don't want any humans here, only robotic delight.

And who cares anyway if a heathen shatters?
Who cares at all, as if any of now matters.
We must aspire to copper lampshades, this is all I know.
In their treacle illumination, we'll forget the long ago.

———◆◆◆———

This poem was performed at Celine's Salon *Zeitgeist* on 27 January 2020 at Gerry's Club, London.

FALLING AWAKE

Daylight falls on the bed.
Eyelashes scrape the pillow.
My body stretches and says thanks.
I thank my legs, torso, arms, face. We are whole.
I sink down, swimming in the duvet and sheet caresses,
unfurling myself.
Warmth cradles my skin, free from pyjamas.
Clouds are on vacation and the blue spreads out, slathered on,
buttering the heavens, as seagulls surf.
Disappearing into this morning's embrace, this melting moment,
absorbed completely, I am sponged up in brightness.
The sun has woken up.

———————◆◆◆━━━━━

This poem was performed at Celine's Salon *Memories and Special Moments* on 28th October 2019 at Gerry's Club, London.

Polly Bull is a queer poet, with a PhD in the history of reading and gender from the University of London. Their first collection, *Outside In*, was published by Wordville Press in 2021.

SASHA & THE SHADES

SMOKE HALLOWS

Take my little soul
You already buried it in a hole
Trees be growing and whispers be blowing
Telling me of freedom I should be knowing
But enough is enough, I will break free
Of these smoke hallows

On the hills where the young souls are sold
And where this great battle shall be fought
I cry this war cry cos I hope you
Spit it out when you die
Die, die, die, die, die

> *Chorus*
> I've got a woman to fight for
> She knows me better than my own damn law
> I've got a woman to fight for
> She knows me better than my own damn law

Find me castles all made out of sand
Greet my old friend silence hand in hand
We got a play date
A lesson in how to love, not to hate

On the hills where young souls are sold
And where this great battle shall unfold
I cry this war cry cos I hope you
Spit it out when you die
Die, die, die, die, die

> I've got a woman to fight for
> She knows me better than my own damn law
> I've got a woman to fight for
> She knows me better than my own damn law
> I've got a woman to fight for
> She knows me better than my own damn law

24

THAT'S THE WAY THAT IT GOES

The crow sings his song, the dog walk begins
Thousand pieces on my floor don't want to let boredom in
Screens flicker whilst the gravy thickens
The sun glistens in your eyes,
whilst the rain dances in the rims of mine

Do I miss ya, I want to kiss ya

> *Chorus*
> I want to know
> But darling that is the way that it goes

Our ambitions fall to the wayside
Your cries dissipate into the wind
Oh darling, oh darling where do we begin

Fathers and sons learn to ride side by side
This is the time to get to know your own king
Minds are crowded but hopefully we shall
become less divided

> *Chorus*
> I want to know
> But darling that is the way that it goes

———————◼◆◆◆◼———————

These songs were performed at Celine's Salon *Where the hell was I last night?* on 14th January 2019 at Gerry's Club, London.

Sasha & The Shades is a band from South East London. Lyrics and lead vocals by Sasha Adamczewski and Eli-Rose Sanford, supported by Tom Julian Jones, Jim Dawkins and Paul Winter-Hart. Their EP, *Grin & Bare It*, is available online.

ZELDA RHIANDO
DORRIE

My story—my story—you stupid woman, and only a poor cracked vessel such as yourself to tell it more's the pity. Start with New York. We'll not speak now of the years before that. I left on a ship, penniless—and came back dressed like a lady, birds in my hat; green, blue, red. Grey silk dress to set it off. They'd never seen the like of it in Dalkey. I looked a million dollars.

We grew up between the wars, and when I saw what was coming I ran away to America. A smart girl could get on there. And I could act refined, even if it was all for show. Mammy would never have us in a mean-looking house. She would be grand even when she didn't have two shillings to rub together. So, we lived in genteel poverty in a big house with too many dusty corners, and sold market eggs as fresh-laid for a few extra pennies. Nine of us rubbing together, legs and arms sprouting out of hand-me-downs, and our father, a commissioned officer, drinking away his past and his future whilst we multiplied before his very eyes—4,6,7,9 strapping children around the big, scarred table in the kitchen. Mammy's castle. And even then, always enough for a skivvy to do for us—for after all weren't we better than them? You'd want to hope so.

Mammy got the place at a peppercorn rent off George Gibson who'd married the auld bitch and had half the county in thrall to him. Once you'd signed on the dotted line you were his creature.

But I'm running away with myself. That was before the war—not the Great War—the war to end all wars. A bare twenty years later here we were again and I wasn't sticking around for this one. Not that Ireland was involved, but all the girls were getting jobs in the textile factories making uniforms, or signing up as nurses; bandaging up some fellow's stinking leg; emptying bedpans. No thank you—not for me!

How did I get here? What was it like on that awful ship, stinking and never quiet; watching your back every minute and never a one you could trust and more fool you if you forget it for even one minute? They'd have your last crust off you as soon as look at you. I was glad I'd taken the time to sew all my worldlies into the seams of my knickers.

And haven't I woken up with hands in my blankets and cursed my luck that I couldn't get a cabin.

And how did I get passage? That's a story—and not a happy one. Did I steal the money? Earn it? (Never!) Was I paid off? Not important now. I got there, didn't I?

New York fooled me. All those glittering jewels in the crown of America. Promises, promises. It was a damn sight harder than that. Than I could have ever believed if I hadn't done it. That I had that in me.

Never you mind.

━━━━◆◆◆━━━━

This story was performed at Celine's Salon *Value* on 12 December 2019 at Gerry's Club, London.

Zelda Rhiando is an Irish writer, and the author of three novels, *Caposcripti*, *Fukushima Dreams* and *Good Morning Mr Magpie*. She lives in Brixton with her husband, two daughters and four cats.

DOUGLAS GRAHAM WILSON

COCKTAIL GAMES

you know how to sophisticate flirtation,
how to sip on a Martini,
play games with passions
and tease.

you know just when to wink
at someone from across a crowded bar—
you know your angles.

to you, it's all a thrilling, complex web—
a challenge—
to ensnare attentions and attractions,
to beguile and seduce.

you know how to work your silhouette—
a hint of muscular legs flexing
beneath tight trousers,
a slight tilt of your broad shoulders,
a languid, nonchalant stretch.

you know how to titillate with your eyes,
imbibing the lustful gazes of your admirers
until you're intoxicated with their craving.

making an entrance is your thing,
but abrupt, solitary exits are your favourite—
and how you exit!

━━━━━ ◆ ◆ ◆ ━━━━━

This poem was performed at Celine's Salon *Nightclubbing* on 6th February 2019 at The Sanctum Hotel, London.

THE TRYING GAME

To Sam –
Love ya!
Douglas x

darling,
your eyebrows are overly plucked
and you're terribly fucked,
making a spectacle of yourself at the bar
and—from what I've observed so far—
I don't think you're going to get laid tonight.

now,
I don't want to be an acerbic bitch
but I can feel an itch in my feet
prompting me to walk over and give you some advice—
I want to be nice—
because I was you a few decades back
and that act never got me what I hoped for.

nobody's gonna save you darling
or put you on the cover of Vogue—
you'll probably just end up in a disappointing apartment
with an equally disappointing rogue.

you see,
it's a delusion,
an illusion you've made up in your mind
and those men hovering around you are all very unkind.

I can see you think you're being fabulous,
but the looks you're getting are incredulous.
and now what?
you're staggering onto the dance floor—
I can't watch anymore.
I'll take this as my cue to
slink out the club door.

———■ ◆ ◆ ◆ ■———

This poem was performed at Celine's Salon *Nightclubbing* on 6th February 2019 at The Sanctum Hotel, London. Originally from Cape Town, Douglas Graham Wilson is a copywriter and spoken word artist based in London.

29

PART FOUR

Santa Semeli
Thomas McColl
Seki Lynch
Ryan Child

SANTA SEMELI

ITS GONNA RAIN NOW

so here it goes
here we are
so here it goes
here we are

everything we held so dear
everything we held as fear

it's gonna rain now
it's gonna rain again
it's gonna rain now
it's gonna rain again
behind the clouds you'll find a brighter light
where all regrets will change to hope
and all bad memories will turn to gold
if i could only make you see
a dream's not only make believe

it's gonna rain now
it's gonna wash away our tears
it's gonna rain now
it's gonna wash away our tears
behind all frowns there lies a smile
i see it lurking and it's mine
if I could pour my heart into your cup
you'd find it easier to forget
but baby wake up
wake up
it's gonna be grand!

DEAR YOU

dear you,
where did i go?
inside a suitcase
out
and
in
there's only
one
tattoo that's on your heart
break
and none can make you feel
what i can do
to you
i am the dream
that did come true
love
love
to sleep
all eyes have shut
i care no more
for you
have left
the way
you
never came
on me
a fading memory
a twisted game
i lost
my tears
you never dried
the garden full of sun
and light
i kissed
your soul
goodnight and morning

moon
and
glory we could have
together it won't be
the way i had
in mind
another kind of child
i promised
friend
her name is fine
and beautiful
like what we had
we've known
your song
and past
regrets are for tomorrow
when we meet
again i know
not
what i
do
to you
to me
how
we will feel
more questions
i can't answer
if you wish
upon a star
signs
are written
in the sky
high
my name
shall rise
and rise
and fall inside your arms

stronger than ever
lasting pleasure
that you owe
my!
world
the oyster
i shall eat me
two times
running faster
than you walk
a way
you can't escape
unless
i want
you
to
stop
wanting

love from,
me.

———◆◆◆———

Both these songs were performed at Celine's Salon *Forbidden Fruit* on 9th January 2017 at The Society Club, London.

Santa Semeli (Semeli Economou) is an actress, director, writer, producer, poet, performer and musician and the founding member of the music group 'Santa Semeli and the Monks'.

THOMAS McCOLL

FRUIT 'N' VEG

The vice squad manned a fruit 'n' veg stall on Berwick Street to trap a fruit fetish ring believed to have been involved in groping grapes, and the elaborate sting ensnared three members doing the strawberry squeeze, the bent banana stroke and the apple shine.

'Arrests only tip of iceberg lettuce,' screamed a tabloid headline. The papers warned this new breed of pervert was determined and astute, and had no trouble finding traders running stalls of ill-repute.

In Soho, one could tell prostitutes had found another service they could sell, when plastic luminous tomatoes replaced red light bulbs in windows.

And it was soon clear that fruit 'n' veg abuse was rife among the clergy too. It got so bad that the Church felt compelled to cancel celebration of the harvest festival, and the Archbishop of Canterbury was moved to make an impassioned plea: 'The Lord has given us fruit 'n' veg, not to play with, but to eat.'

The vice squad even had to arrest two bobbies on the beat: They were found sat in the lounge of a pub which had a back room where an illegal fruit 'n' veg show had only moments before been in full swing, and though claiming they'd entered the premises simply to hand out anti-knife crime leaflets, the officers had trouble explaining why each had a cucumber attached to his belt in place of his truncheon.

And it wasn't just police, but judges, lawyers and prominent politicians getting caught. It seemed like the very fabric of society was falling apart, and the PM's response was quick. He brought in severe penalties for fruit 'n' vegploitation. In a speech, he made it clear: 'If you abuse the carrot. you get the stick!'

SPRINGTIME IN SOHO

Anyone walking through Soho in winter cannot miss that, even in a telephone box that's dark and dank and stinks of piss, it's somehow always spring.

All year round, each day of the week, lust germinates and flowers into blooms: flimsy pieces of card, with blu-tack roots, so weak they never last much more than a couple of hours.

The prospects for survival of this species would be bleak if it wasn't for all the hovering men.

Just off Brewer Street, inside a telephone box cocoon, a man's already mutated into something that his wife would never recognise: a strange hybrid creature, with a human face but a pair of bulging compound eyes...

...a husband, driven no longer by mutual love and respect but by the single-mindedness of an insect.

And, all over Soho, the same thing's happening too to scores of other men, ensuring that tomorrow it will start all over again...

———————◆◆◆———————

Both these pieces were performed at Celine's Salon *Seven Deadly Sins* on 3rd February 2016 at The Society Club, London.

Thomas McColl first read at Celine's Salon back in 2016. His latest collection is *Grenade Genie* (Fly on the Wall Press, 2020).

SEKI LYNCH

THE FEAST

When I dream, I dream of you. All of you
I dream of a great table. A banquet in the forest
I dream of Xenia and of every guest playing host
A billion hands cooking favoured dishes
Laced with laughter, pricked and peppered with spices
Salted with tears, stocks thickened with blood
And of course you're there too, as I knew you would be—
Eyes dizzy with love

The great banquet table
Laid with porcelain jugs fashioned as fish
Mosaic plates of familiar patterns
Cutlery which fits as if smithed for bearer's hands
Napkins of fine linen—at a touch—we remember other lives

Usually so careful of words
I dream of you and they pour from me
In hearing these, your own thoughts spill out
The banquet is our secret and our telling of it
Reunited, the dogs in our chests curl upon themselves
To settle flop-eared into their corners of the heart

Already the wine is flowing
I slip out unnoticed among the bustling
The dancing and the singing
In the forest-garden I slow by the waterfall
Which is breathing in the silence of the moonlight
Far from the gathering; only the tender water's hushing
As it tries to restrain the excitement of meeting with itself
In the water's mirrored tryst - the sohbet of the party

Back at the feast
A furnace of mingling and flirting and charms exchanged
Essential metal is being formed
Each guest is alchemist and mineral
Polished mirror and reflected gold

As we eat we begin to forget
We forget our age and begin to lose our accents
When asked, we can't recall our favourite song
We forget our names and the names of our beloveds
We forget our self-consciousness and our scars
Empty and full, our laugher flows
We forget ourselves and clamber onto the table
The wine too flows and we guests begin to embrace
We merge as fire meets fire
In reuniting we realise we were never apart
A foot tips a candle; the tablecloth catches
We are the threads and the flames
A drunken inferno

And this is not a dream
We are awake, not dreaming
This is not a dream
We are awake, not sleeping
Time has been an inside joke between heartbeats
There is no light or dark; we have no need for these things here
Here there is no sound because that is not how fire makes music
Life has been a dream and we are unformed crystals ringing
Once again we have no mouths and we are singing
Crackling into ever-being
Empty and full as flames

———•♦•———

This poem was performed at Celine's Salon *Dreams* on 11th March 2021 on YouTube. Seki Lynch is a literary creative. Find his heart-shaped consciousness trails wandering the Internet. He is the author of *Ten Drinks that Changed the World*, published by ACC Art Books in 2018.

RYAN CHILD

THE BOY IN THE WOLF SUIT

Packed up... like the inside of an egg
though he was more quiet white than tasty BRIGHT yellow
(the best part, right?)

Until the idea clicked
like a key in a lock
or the endless chimes and heavy tick tocks
of the clock... in his ears
Flanked by the unloveliest molls
sucking at the fizz of freshly cracked beers
his mission was clear

Long fingers searching for needle and thread
(picture this part happening under a strobe light)
Planning, sketching, sewing, ripping, tearing, wrenching, gluing,
moulding
Something dazzling
awe-inspiring
all together life-changing
worth more than the crowns of a million fabled kings.

Red as the work of a rose's prick
and grey as the drench of wet-heavy brick
bigger claws than any male or female,
than the meat on Old Street,
the posh tarts of Green Park
the proud cocks of Camden Lock
or the ones that bring blushes and impure thoughts to the neon road of
Tottenham Court.

And as the hands and lips of girls and boys
made their way through traffic and noise
to find the Boy in the Wolf Suit like a magnet,
declaring love, reciting sonnets in his honour,
they needn't have bothered.

He slashed through their smiles
and ripped at their shoulders,
severed their heads and threw them like boulders
into the Thames.

He buried his face in ribcages and stomachs,
sucked on hearts like a greedy toddler, with a gobstopper
or a compulsive bubble-wrap popper

UNABLE. TO. STOP.

So he chugged at their blood as though it were water
amid the wreck of his mass slaughter
NEVER DONE, chewing up lungs for fun
Gnawing at bones, along Charing Cross Road, all the way home

But more came, and still they chased him

They screamed 'TAKE MY INSIDES! YOU'RE TOO BEAUTIFUL TO
LOSE! WE WANT YOU SO BADLY! WE NEED TO GET INSIDE OF
YOU!'

But the Boy in the Wolf Suit backed away
and ran as though his belly wasn't filled with a bloody wealth.

———————◗ ◆ ◆ ◗———————

These poems were performed at Celine's Salon *Seven Deadly Sins* on 2nd
March 2016 at The Society Club, London.

AFTER 6

After 6 we go on the clock. Leoric is always quiet and sickly smug because his regular, who actually brings him flowers, arrives every other night at 6:15 sharp and holes up with him for most of the night, even though Sinch told me that all they really do is snuggle and read.

He told me as a sorry because I caught him stealing my cigarettes, and when I laughed he put his forehead to mine, but he still didn't give them back.

It's kept too warm in here because Vincent says that February is being mean. I touch half-there snow on the shoulders of the coats hanging heavy in the hall, but Vincent catches me and thinks I'm after wallets, shooing me away and I scramble back to the hotbox living room, quick as a cat might.

It's hard not to sleep. Even when you know you're being shopped from behind the two-way mirror that Vincent put in special. Everything looks red and the TV is never off. Vincent kept the Christmas lights up because he said we looked better in the dimishness. He actually used the word dimishness and snapped a finger at my eyebrow that moved upwards all on its own. Edie-Boy laughed too but Vincent didn't see.

Edie-Boy is everyone's favourite and I don't even care. He says he hasn't noticed but I know he likes it. I said it to him the night he came into my room and made shadow animals on the wall. He didn't say a word but I saw the baby of a smile at his lips.

The twins aren't really twins. Vincent just sells them that way. One time, this guy, we called him the priest because he wore one of those collars, but none of us believed he was for real, fell to the floor in front of them and began talking in tongues. Vincent threw him out, but since then the twins always claimed that the baptism they received that night had kept them fresh of face and disease-free.

Everyone just rolled their eyes, chewing their mouths from the inside.

He's not mad with me anymore, Vincent.

The tips I kept from him, the ones I hide in one of the rollerskates he bought me, that I never use, he found them, I don't know how. He screamed about my disloyalty and my laziness. This was earlier, and outside was already telling us it was night, so I guess he knew he couldn't make the walls shake. Instead he tied me off, I felt the scratch, then nothing... and by the time it was after 6, all I knew was that the rollerskate was empty and it was my turn to shower.

After we're done, when the doorbell stops ringing and the red of the living room dies to some weird grey, Edie-Boy falls down next to me on my bed.

He says not to worry, that pretty soon, he and I will turn into pigeons like the ones lined up along the edge of the roof, high up here. He says that we'll get fat on the food thrown out by the nice restaurants further along the street and when it gets too cold we can sleep in the old drums no longer used by the Royal Opera because he knows where they keep them and he knows a way in.

"Pigeons?' I ask.

"Pigeons," he says, making a bird with his hands that flies along my wall to where the morning comes in.

➤ ◆ ◆ ◆ ⬛

This story was performed at Celine's Salon *Bad Behaviour* on 5th April 2016 at The Society Club. London.

Ryan Child lives in Central London. He regularly performs spoken word around the city.

INTERVAL

PART FIVE

One Voice, One Cello & A Mad Belgian
NaMo
Gis Harris
Jo Danzig
Steven Appleby

ONE VOICE, ONE CELLO & A MAD BELGIAN

WHISKEY JOE

I met a man called Whiskey Joe while cycling down the road,
It's like a sort of habit, I suppose.
He took me for a drink or two but when he went to pay,
(then I had a blackout, then I had a blackout).
'Precision is the enemy of art,' he said to me.
'And dedication puts you in a hole,
So, let's hit the town and spread around this tender then you'll see:
What's lurking at the deepest darkest corners at the bottom of your
soul!'

> *Chorus:*
> Whiskey Joe and his eight pound notes
> As colourful as his anecdotes
> He's the man that you need him to be
> Everybody takes them, very strange,
> He doesn't care about his two pound change
> He's the man that you need him to be,
> If you want to be free.

I looked upon the money that he used to pay the bar
These lovely multi-coloured eight pound notes
'You can buy them for a tenner,' is what he explained to me
(Then I had a blackout, then I had a blackout)
'The two pounds change is worth it for the pleasure that they bring,
And everyone accepts them with a smile.
A little bit of elbow grease will make the world go round.'
I'd like to hang around this world a while.

Chorus:
Whiskey Joe and his eight pound notes
As colourful as his anecdotes
He's the man that you need him to be
Everybody takes them, very strange,
He doesn't care about his two pound change
He's the man that you need him to be,
If you want to be free.

———■ ♦ ♦ ♦ ■———

This song was performed on Celine's Salon *Dreams* YouTube show on 11th March 2021.

Lyrics by Rupert Gillett. One Voice, One Cello & A Mad Belgian is a unique collaboration between jazz-cellist and singer/songwriter Rupert Gillett and soprano saxophonist, melodeon player and singer/songwriter Jennifer El Gammal.

NaMo
THE FIRE SPIRIT

It had been raining for one year, seven months and ten days.

As the coach dipped into the inclined approach to the first village of the inundated Cauca Valley, a few short miles to the North East of Santiago De Cali, a swirling torrent lapped at the lower lip of the lurching vehicle's grimy windows forming a fluid connective plane to the doorways of abandoned white adobe houses through which bobbing furniture and household items could be glimpsed.

Deliriously fatigued after a night of prolonged hypnagogia, I was still finding it hard to dislodge the jarring images of the previous day. Foremost, how the benign expression of ingenuous kindliness on the elderly lady's face had contorted into one of revulsion as the greenish brown, two-foot snake escaped her mouth, to drop coiling into the pink plastic receptacle at her feet.

'The little miracles of daily life constructed by love.'

The light frequency of Luz's words fleetingly achieved the dominant signal on the dial of cerebral random radio before the tenebrous broadcast of reminiscence resumed.

The white robed curandero had sent those of us under maleficios into a spartan annex furnished simply with chairs, each with a bucket before it, arranged in a wide arc. I took my place on an empty seat and, with the help of my companion José, an affable and elegant young astrophysics student with dreams of Oxford, did as we had been instructed, and as others were doing. A rationalist with a generous sense of the esoteric, he had humoured me by accompanying me here. Bespectacled and pressed-shirted José would pour jugs of water into my mouth, my head tipped back, in order to try and flush out the 'manifestation'. Within minutes a disoriented young man in the next chair was coughing up a sodden mouse into his bucket. Three chairs away it was a large, hideous spider-like creature that flopped into the receptacle. The occupant of a further seat eructated a huge fur ball rather like that which a cat might produce.

To further embroider the chimerical proceedings; snotty, sodden and gagging as I was, a pair of dusky, silicone-enhanced creatures had arranged themselves alluringly before me. Exotic narco wives attempting to seduce me, insisting I gave them my phone number even as I was being 'water-boarded'.

Since no entity would allow itself to be flushed out of me, I made an entreaty to José to cease. I could take no more choking and was becoming concerned about my blood:water ratio. The curandero gave me a sachet of purging powders, telling me it still remained for me to wrest the manifestation out upon my return to Medellin. He insisted that the trabajo had been laid upon me two years previously in Rio de Janeiro, land of macumba and candomblé, and was increasing in strength.

'How could such creatures live inside a human body?' I posed the question.

'Those are not animals.' The curandero turned back to me. 'Let's just say they are manifestations of evil.'

The energy within the suburban house used for the ritual was unlike any I had ever experienced—a thick, dark, supercharged, mucilaginous fug. But I had most certainly felt the presence of light there also. It was perplexing.

'Do NOT answer your phone if the narco women call you,' José instructed me several times. 'They want to fuck you, and that'll end up getting you killed!'

My phone started vibrating almost immediately. Boy, were they magnificent. As so many narco women were. I reluctantly refrained from picking up.

'The little miracles of daily life constructed by love.'

I mentally caressed Luz's words. I needed to move into the light after orbiting such profound darkness. I knew I had to get to The Tree of Life when I reached Medellin.

The intercity bus finally climbed out of the deluged lowlands. Some eight hours later, after having traversed the winding estradas of the heavily-forested mountains south of Medellin, we began the decent into that city. Lolling in a hypnopompic state, I dreamed of Luis Fernando, the wheelchair-bound child-in-a-man's-body in the mountains of San Pedro de los Milagros. Another curandero, who, weeks previously, had removed the insect that resembled no other species on earth from my abdomen in spiritual surgery.

'This is just a messenger, there's more to draw out,' he had congenially announced.

And I remembered how his countenance had changed from childlike to demonic in the blink of an eye, spitting salacious words in a gargoylesque hiss, before at once regaining innocence. I awoke abruptly and fully.

I had barely slipped the key into my front door when I knew. My apartment had been robbed. The skylight was open—everything except my passport and a small amount of money gone.

At The Tree of Life, Luz served up her improvised gourmet vegan cuisine, which she could never repeat a second time.

'We'll finish what you have sought to do,' her husband Sergio reassured me.

Recently returned from a week-long Gurdjieff retreat in Cali, he appeared gaunt, was three kilos lighter, but noticeably spiritually reinforced. I felt warm and at ease in their company as I did in the embosoming environs of The Tree of Life.

After the simple yet sumptuous repast, a short drive to the neighbouring barrio and we found ourselves in Luz's high-walled house. I was instructed to take a specially prepared bath in a tub infused with fragrant herbs, slip on a simple, fresh, white cotton garment, then to make my appearance in the spacious, high-ceilinged living room where Sergio and Luz had delineated a circle, some three metres in diameter, upon the wooden floor. Also attired in white, they motioned for me to position myself in the exact centre.

I was entirely unprepared for what happened next. Producing a lighter, Luz crouched and set alight whatever substance constituted the circle. The flame jumped to the height of my shoulders in an instant; then drew like a curtain to surround me entirely. I found myself within a perfect circle of uniform white fire.

As Luz and Sergio began an incantation, almost inaudible through the flames, my initial apprehension gave way to calm deference. Within the ring I felt time lose its influence. Feeling exhaustion and wishing to close my eyes, turned to elation and lightness.

Out of the corner of my eye I glimpsed small eddies disturbing the uniformity of the flames. As the vortexes evolved into larger tornadoes to the right of my field of vision, I caught Sergio's eye. He motioned me to turn around. I glanced over my right just in time to see a larger disturbance, a form of roughly human height, making its surreptitious exit through the flames.

———◆◆◆———

Barrio—neighbourhood
Candomblé—syncretic religion involving the manifestation of Orixás.
Curandero—traditional native healer/shaman in Latin America.
Macumba—a folk religion practiced in Brazil involving sorcery
Maleficios—evil spells or curses
Narco—cocaine dealer/smuggler
Trabajo—literally 'work' but, in this context, a curse or magic spell
Gurdjieff—an Armenian mystic

———◆◆◆———

This story was performed at Celine's Salon on Soho Radio, London. Currently residing in South East Asia, NaMo, is an analogue, pre-industrial, raw, vegetarian, melomaniac, sapiosexual, natural-healing, bibliophile, somnambulist escape artist.

GIS HARRIS

SHE SLEEPS ON A FEATHER'S EDGE

Softly laying on the side of my dream,
Carp swimming in the sky.
Ponder little on the wheres or the why.

Particle resistance in a quantum existence, what was that out of the
side of my eye?

She sleeps on a feather's edge
Lush folds of love, caught by the web of a spider's glove.
Bitten, bleeding and ready for feeding
Over the edge, after the shove.

Home, it feels so far away, no ruby slippers.
Run from the hand that hides in the chequers.
Deny it, look into the distance, awake from your dream on the edge of
feathers.

———➤ ♦ ♦ ◄———

This poem was performed on Celine's Salon *Dreams* YouTube show on 11th
March 2021.

IS THERE LIFE ON MARS?

Is there life on Mars? If there are they are not driving cars.
A mere pebble, the red one, a cold lonely dead one.
Was there life?
Are we right, to spend and send robots up into the night?
33.9 million miles, looking for death, drilling with diamonds
powered by black solar tiles.
'There was water,' they'd say. 'We oughta go and then stay.
There is no coming back anyway.'
Mars, you are so far, desolate, suffocated with dust.
Jump into our rockets for die there we must.
Alone on a rock, abandoned, forgot. There is no water nor food,
We are left there to rot.
The bones get buried, over time fossilized
Then more travellers arrive searching their prize.
Jim looks at Harry gazing out at the stars,
'You know what, Jim? Really missing my car!'
'Ahhh fuck that, Harry, is there life on Mars?'

———————◆◆◆———————

This poem was performed on Celine's Salon *Is There Life on Mars?*
YouTube show on 8th April 2021.

Gis Harris is a 52-year-old skateboarding surrealist artist from Hayle in
deepest Cornwall, loving life and the ever-inspiring landscape and people
of west Cornwall.

JO DANZIG
MY GRANDMA SANDRA

My Grandma Sandra always had this faded plastic bangle on her wrist. As a child I loved that bracelet and watched the bits of red glitter move in the gel.

Over the years, the bangle yellowed—the plastic hardened and the gel became opaque until the glitter no longer swam around the circumference, much like Sandra's veins that could barely shuffle her down the road.

One day my dad said, 'get that filthy bracelet off your wrist before you die in it.'

'Get your hand off it—Bill gave me that and it isn't going anywhere. I'm not and what have you ever got me?'

'I'll get you a McDonalds if you want?'

'I can get my own.' And with that she heaved her little pudding body up from the bedframe and got her purse, the old-fashioned kind with just one clip.

'Come on Joanne, we are going for an outing.' And she grabbed my hand.

Golders Green High Street was always busy. We walked our way through the crowds of Jewish youths waiting for bagels and salt beef. We were Jewish but not that kind of Jewish.

Not organised or dressed for a Saturday night.

Sarah Gwiazda Starr liked to be known as Sandra Sutton—the woman who ate burgers and drank Emva Cream until she slumped outside the chemist and someone had to walk her home. They thought she had a son.

Under her bed we found some hundred empty cartons.

Some alive with maggots and her room twinkled with cheap sherry bottles.

I don't know what happened to the bangle.

———————◆◆◆◄———————

This poem was performed for Celine's Salon *Icons* on 3rd December 2018 at Gerry's Club, London.

THE CRYSTAL FROG

Hours sat by her bedside listening to Barbara Streisand, the sound
giving some distant familiar comfort.
When I cut her finger nails, they came off in my hand
The life force joining skin to bone already saying its goodbyes
Unable to speak, she physically detached herself from this world
before our eyes.
We imagined her thoughts and pain and wondered if she could feel our
love.

When I moved the pillows to do something useful, the air dispelled
from her fragile lungs
The soles of her feet, like sandpaper on dry wood, scraped against the
sheets
Her skin could be lifted from her frame, connecting tissue withered in
illness.

As Christmas approached, we wondered if we should buy gifts for the
shell that was our mother
Would she know?
Would she see?
Would she blink her eyes in recognition?
It seemed weird to do so but wrong not to.

As the day approached my brother came with a small crystal colour-
changing frog
And from her loving granddaughter—who was sick as she kissed her
fading Nana,
A small black felt cat.

———— ♦ ♦ ♦ ————

This poem was performed for Celine's Salon *Icons* on 3rd December 2018 at
Gerry's Club, London.

Jo grew up as an only child between two parents, two houses and two
countries. To make sense of the world she started writing down memories of
the people and events that shaped her experience. This is the first time Jo has
submitted her work for print.

STEVEN APPLEBY

PITY ME

Meanwhile, in another part of the city, I'm thinking about the butcher and the baker, about meat and dough. The butcher's hands are juicy, like steak, and feel reassuringly strong when he holds me. The baker smells of milk and his sweat tastes sweet. He is giving me as a present to the butcher but can't decide whether to bake me inside a cake as a surprise or use me as a cake decoration. He starts by pushing me into the cake, dough squeezing up between my legs, to see how that will work. Then he changes his mind, licks me clean and places me on top next to a sleazy, cake decoration bridegroom. The bridegroom has sugar lips and a hard, candy cock, which may come in useful later.

As he works the baker talks, telling me a story about the age of darkness.

'Once upon a time,' he says. 'Probably in the past, or maybe in the future—whenever it was that the world was going to Hell so fast that the Devil himself could hardly keep up—there was a little district of the city called Pity Me.'

'Pity Me. That's where we live now.'

'Yes, honey. Though it's changed a bit. Nowadays Pity Me isn't too terrible to look at, or live in, despite its name, but in those days, whenever they were, the people were awoken every night by shouts and cries as the Devil went past pushing his handcart piled high with the damned. But despite this, and the fact that nothing grew properly there and, when healthy things arrived, they soon waned and withered and died. Despite all this, Pity Me was criss-crossed by narrow streets lined with small, grey, detached houses where people like you and me lived. They had little gardens front and back planted up with dead things and washing lines. There was a small, ash-grey, soot-covered park; a few shops, lit up during the day by tarnished yellow electric light, and a few factories backing onto the canal, into which they tipped their dirty water and anything else they'd used up and didn't want any more. The days in Pity Me were never fully light and the nights never fully dark, so a life spent in Pity Me was a life lived in permanent dusk.

On one of the streets, in a grey house just like all the others, lived a baby boy with his cute, sensible mommy and his wild, crazy daddy. The daddy was sterile and set fire to buildings for a living. The mommy, knowing that the daddy knew he was sterile, lived in constant fear. But the daddy seemed to love the baby boy, or at least to like him, since he paid him no attention at all. So, the baby boy loved his mommy and his daddy and life carried along in a truce of shopping, burning buildings and walks to the park.

One particular night—night according to the clock, since, as I said before, the light is much the same all the twenty-four hours long due to the fires and smoke and whatnot—the daddy arrives home from work covered in soot as usual, except that tonight he is burning inside. The mommy can see the hot coals glowing out from deep inside his tired, grey, ash-coloured eyes. Without a word, the daddy picks up the baby boy, puts him in his pram and pushes him out of the door. When the mommy starts putting on her coat to follow, the daddy says;

'Get supper ready.'

Then he goes, slamming the door behind him. The mommy hears the key turn in the lock and through the window sees the daddy disappear down the street in the opposite direction to the park. The mommy looks in the daddy's bag and sees that he has brought home only enough supper for two, so she feels for her front door key but it isn't in her pocket, then she looks for the spare front door key but it isn't on the hook. Feeling panic, as if the fire inside the daddy has started a second little fire in her breast, the mommy opens the sitting room window and climbs out into the garden, snapping the dead grass as she lands and leaving dead footprints across the lawn. She hurries up the street in the direction the daddy went but she can't see him, and the little fire inside her starts to crackle as it catches and begins to blaze.

The next street is empty, and so is the next, and now there are cross streets and side streets and where, in Pity Me, could the daddy have disappeared to so quickly? Then the mommy sees the damp marks of pram wheels leaving a puddle of ash and petrol heading towards Coal Street, and she hurries on. Up ahead a building is on fire—are those the daddy's friends? Is this where he's gone? The flames burning inside the mommy's chest start to roar, as if doused in paraffin, but no, these men work for a rival company which is bigger and busier than the daddy's, causing him to shout and complain and hit the wall, leaving the prints of his fists in soot to be cleaned off later. The mommy hurries round the corner and there, up ahead, stands the daddy next to the pram. Just staring into the canal where the short street ends at a wharf. Just standing. Just staring.

'Where's the baby?' screams the mommy, 'What the fuck have you done with my baby?!'

The daddy turns, pauses for a moment as if he might have something to say, then he smiles a little smile, which is unusual for him, because he doesn't smile very much, and pushes the pram into the canal.

The mommy howls, like tearing metal, and runs straight into the canal, fighting her way through the thick, waist-deep water to the pram, but it's empty.

Across the other side of the canal stands a fisherman. He is casting a specially weighted hook into the thick water. The weights are heavy so they'll carry the hook through the crust on top of the water down to the bottom, otherwise it would just sit on the surface. The fisherman is annoyed by the noise the woman is making, and the splashing, because it will attract the big fish. These big fish eat the smaller ones he's trying to catch. He sees the top of the water lurch up a little, then fall again, as if the water is breathing. He sees little tremors spread across it. The big fish are almost here. Then the fisherman feels a pull on his line. A bite! Just in time! He reels in the hook and yes, there's something... But it's the wrong shape. And it's coughing.

The mommy looks and sees her baby boy hanging from the fisherman's line. As she wades towards him she feels a little tickle behind one calf. Then another tickle, like a kiss, behind the other. Then a searing pain... and she is gone.'

The baker pauses and looks at me, encased in my fluffy, white, icing sugar dress standing there on his cake next to the groom, and he smiles and says - as he always does after telling this tale,

'That baby was you, honey. That's how I caught you and that's how you came to live here, with me.'

━━━━◆◆◆◼━━━

This story was performed at Celine's Salon on Soho Radio, London.
This piece was written before Steven started the graphic novel, *Dragman*. The whole book grew out of the tone and some of the ideas that appear in this early draft.

Steven Appleby is an absurdist cartoonist and artist. He has created work for newspapers, books, radio, television, gallery exhibitions, the stage— and even Pixies's album *Trompe le Monde*. He lives, works and daydreams in London.

PART SIX

Louisa Young
Rachel Dreyer
Ashley Chapman
Cathy Flower
Andrew Brown

LOUISA YOUNG

JUST BECAUSE YOU'RE STRONG

Just because you're strong don't mean it's easy
Just because you cry don't make you weak
Just because I'm here don't mean I love you
If I'm quiet that don't mean that you can't speak

Just because I'm in your arms don't make me a fool for you
Just because we want to doesn't mean we should
Every time we meet there's something going on
Something going wrong, something true

I see you being strong and strong and strong again
I'd like to be
Something good for you
Something good for you

I know there's things that you've got going on
I know there's things, nothing to do with me
I know about you
How it's not easy, what you're going through
It's not nothing, what you're going through

Just because you're strong don't mean it's easy
Just because you cry don't make you weak
Just because I'm here don't mean I love you
If I'm quiet that don't mean that you can't speak

I see you being strong and strong and strong again
I'd like to be
Something good for you
Something good for you
Something good for you
Something good for you

YOU LEFT EARLY (and you left alone)

You waltz in your coat-tail flying, cool as an angel without trying
You're at the piano, knowing every song
Billie and Cole, all night long
You laugh and flirt with all the women, smoke their cigarettes,
love their singing
They could never leave you alone
You played so late and we sang along
We all knew that you drank twice your share in half the time
It's blazoned all around your soul like a neon sign
You lit the night I ain't lying when you stayed late and we played
along
I'd 'a been your silver lining, bold and bright and shining
I'd 'a brought you safely home—but you left early, and you left
alone

You danced with all the gorgeous women, broke their hearts and
left 'em swimming
In lakes of their own tears at your heart of stone
When after all you leave alone
We all knew you drank—twice your share in half the time
You had it hanging tight around your neck like a ball and chain
Day and night, I ain't lying
Then you left early, and you left alone
I was to be your silver lining, strong and bright, both of us shining
We were gonna bring each other home—then you left early
and you left alone

BRARIA, or They've Changed the Bloody Design

I'm going to buy some new bras
The same kind I've been wearing for years.
They're supportive and black
and just right for my back
It's a marvellous simple design.

I'm going to purchase brassières
The kind I've been wearing for years
Of course Marks and Spencers
But uh-oh—no chance, as
They've changed the bloody design

They've changed the bloody design
It's a vast misogynist crime
The balconette's lovely and fits like a glove this action is scarcely benign!
Those horrible flat-chested swine
I've gone into an awful decline
Since John Galliano leaned over my piano and told me tits spoil the line
They've changed the bloody design

I don't want lace, I don't want flowers,
I don't want to try everything on, it takes hours
I know 32 H is rather extreme
(I rather think it's just me, and the Queen)
I relied on that bra cos it makes me feel fine
And now they've changed the bloody design

I was looking for proper upholstery
But nothing too horridly bolstery
Underwires ARE desired,
And strong straps required
But they've changed the bloody design

I don't want strapless, I don't want padding,
I don't want peekaboo for extramarital gadding
Chicken fillets are not de rigeur
(they do zilch for my kind of figeur...)
I just want a bra that will keep them in place
(or a little bit higher, and nearer my face)
I just want a bra that will keep them in line
But they've changed the bloody design.

I was going to buy some new bras
The same kind I'd been wearing for years
They were black and supportive
but the mission's abortive
They've changed the bloody design

They've changed the bloody design
It's a vast misogynist crime
The balconette's lovely and fits like a glove we DON'T NEED this absurd redesign
Their intentions are surely malign
To purchase I'm now disinclined
Since dear Mary Portas declared me a shortarse I've formed a bra-shop picket line!
'cos
They've changed the bloody design
Yes
They've changed the bloody design
Oh God
They've changed the bloody design

———————◼ ◆ ◆ ◼———————

These songs were performed at Celine's Salon *Memories and Special Moments* on 28th October 2019 at Gerry's Club, London.

Louisa Young is a writer and songwriter. Her eleven novels include the award-winning *My Dear I Wanted to Tell You* trilogy. She's half of the children's author Zizou Corder (with her daughter Isabel Adomakoh Young), and half of the band 'Birds of Britain' (with Alex Mackenzie).

RACHEL DREYER

TOKYO STORY

With only a month in Tokyo, and serious student financial woes, my goal was to clear as many debts as I could without ending up underneath some sweaty businessman.

Swim in a giant fish tank dressed as a mermaid? Be a police woman in Arrest Bar? I chose hostessing in the tiny club Glamour. This situation vacant, I anticipated, would be a vacant situation indeed. The lights were low—to hide the dust and because people look good in the dark. Tables for two with vinyl cloths and fake candles, surrounded a tiny dance floor below a red tinsel stage.

An English woman, Karen, showed me around. 'I've been hostessing 17 years—my liver's fucked,' she complained, struggling into a lurex boob tube.

Our aim was to get exhausted businessmen to buy as much champagne as possible. The trick was to pour most of it away unnoticed.

The arrival of each customer was announced by disco lights and the playing of a macabre little tune, more suitable to a fairground. This signalled girls to convene like lost cattle on the dance floor, where they attempted to dance alluringly. Elderly Mamasan described the beauties, 'Tiffany—she is a student from Sweden, very lovely girl....' (Never the truth. 'Mercedes, a divorced mother of two with an aggressive attitude and a face full of fillers.')

Karen explained ways to cultivate a party atmosphere with customers. I could excuse myself briefly, tip my champagne down the ladies-room sink, and refill with ginger ale; identical in the glass. Champagne was discretely tipped into artificial plants, the shag pile carpet, just about anywhere. 'See that girl there?'—tip on the floor—'I've heard she sleeps with the owner's wife'—splash—'has an extra nipple'—pour in the potted palm.

I was the spoilt, wild, Western party girl! Campai! I flicked my hair and threw my head back. Mr Hirohito's jokes were so funny it hurt. If he wanted to sing karaoke, I encouraged something heavy metal. Breathless in his presence, aroused to movement by his song, onstage I'd writhe around him.

Club rules were strict though, no surprise in an industry drawing some heritage from the Geisha tradition. We wore long dresses, and berated errant customers. My new Japanese was mainly, 'Dame Dame!' (Stop, stop), or 'Hatchucashi Nei' (you can't do that here), to the misdemeanour of a hand on the knee. But, for one hostess, the rules seemed not to apply.

Tara was an elegant red head in her mid-twenties, haughty with customers and rarely socialising with other girls. Despite Tara's aloof demeanour, devotees would wait all evening, and scamper off crestfallen if she failed to appear.

'They say crime doesn't pay,' she whispered coolly one night. 'I think they're wrong.'

'I never have sex for free,' she boasted another evening, as she admired her reflection in the dressing room mirror. But I knew her smitten suitors were attracted mainly to the crystal meth which she dispensed in tiny bags.

Sometimes, if a customer grew too insistent with another girl, Tara would swoop in like a crow at a carcass and lure him away, his ears red with promises.

She'd peel off a trail of clothing from the hotel room door to the bed, then extract a large fee from her Romeo. He'd bask in smug anticipation while she went to freshen up, sure she wouldn't flee barefoot in bra and knickers through the lobby of the Shangri La.

Meanwhile in the locked bathroom, shower running, Tara pulled on a dress and some ballet pumps from her bag. Scooping up her jacket, clippity clop, she was gone. In this grindingly sleazy world, there was something almost heroic about our wily one that got away.

It was usually best to bashfully decline propositions, but extortionate dinner dates yielded hostesses' hefty commissions. Men we dragged into the club meant pennies from heaven, dispensed with each arrival.

The new girl, Shimrit, was unwilling to drink, and sat sulking an arm's-length from her customers, earning herself the moniker of Prim Shim.

She grabbed my arm in the Rappongi night-club district one evening, 'help me—it's my customer!"

I imagined him in a gaudily decorated love hotel, his heart imploded from bad cocaine.

'I got him too drunk,' she wailed. 'He's in the bathroom and the staff can't open the door!'

Shimrit had clearly over-egged the pudding, and the pudding lay heavy on the toilet floor.

'Help me carry him to the club to get my fee!' she begged.

For a moment I considered this—two Western girls and an unconscious accountant—even if we carried him, would a taxi actually pick us up? In the harsh light of the bathroom, with the salivating salaryman at our feet, I'd suddenly had enough. 'Shimrit! There's a line, and we've crossed it!'

We left him in a nearby cubicle hotel, glasses on side table, with his wallet if not his dignity intact.

Dull conversation for 70 hours per week, fake laughs and tedium were clearly getting to Shimrit and to me too. I'd willingly been swallowed up by Tokyo's nightlife, but the hilarity of taking the low road had passed, and London beckoned once more. But I'd enjoyed this indulgent flight of fancy, with an amused curl on my lip.

———◆◆◆———

This story was performed at Celine's Salon *Rebellion* on 14th June 2017 at The Society Club, London. Rachel Dreyer is a writer, DJ and music producer, now living in New Zealand.

ASHLEY CHAPMAN

THE BOHOS OF SOHO

We start in Greek Street.
Not any night,
But a grand finale;
Last orders,
At The Coach & Horses,
Before the corporate boyz move
On the pub where inky Boho Jeffrey Bernard drank,
And Gary, the actor, and his mates are on the piss.

Meanwhile, a mum runs her hands
Though my strands.
'Tell me everything,' she thrills, 'about your hair.'
But there's nothing to say:
I barely wash it,
Never brush it,
And only finger comb it.
But she carries on in my locks,
Then off to dinner with her bloke.

We head off to Trisha's at 57,
A lively basement heaven:
In energy, in noise, in smoke.
I chat with Mark.
Got his heart broke:
It's hard,
When love fucks up,
To sever those traumatic bonds;
Thick as pillar posts.
Goodbye, the cocktail of toxicity,
That had you high,
The sex, the texts, the tenderness,
And, shit, the love.

Kass, a boxer musician, comes
And shakes our hands.
He's in Armani,
And says,
His eyes little dark raisins,
'I prefer a poet over a bruiser.'
And, 'I don't fight no more,
If I did—so I don't bother—
I'd kill 'em.'

In the corner,
Two girls with dreamy eyes,
So I read 'em love poems.

Then Jessica's head pops round the door.
We hug and swap tales:
'I'm all messed up,' I tell her.
'What not her, the one you wrote that poem for?'
'My man,' she confides,
'All crazy passion and wild sex for months—
Then nothing.
Just fizzled out like it was never meant to be.'

She exits.

'You alright Gary?'
'Yeah, you?'
'Fine.'
But I don't buy him a beer,
A bottle of Peroni is £5.
'No, it's £3,' he says, 'if you pay cash.'
I head for the bar.
Three times I explain to the barman:
'It's £3 cash.'

'Who told you that?'

'Gary,' I say defensively.

'Well, tell Gary,' he says, slamming the bottle down, 'if he doesn't shut the fuck up,

He'll be paying a fiver, too.'

A young American artist Kirsty starts talking to me.

She's trying to get ahead in art,

And says that when she was a kid,

On a blazing Tuscany night filled with stars,

She walked out onto a stone balustrade balcony,

And knew, in that moment,

She was no longer her mom and dad,

But herself, Kirsty.

The boxer musician shoves a tall fellow hard against the wall.

The altercation

Is over before it starts.

Mark buys me a drink.

Kirsty goes to the toilet.

Kass gives me a wolfish smile.

The corner girls have gone.

Mark slips off his stool.

Gary and I linger

With a feisty young bar lady,

Serving the Bohos of Soho.

Drinking in their pathos,

Exhaling in the shadows,

Mingling in their juices.

The Bohos of Soho.
Ahhh, the Bohos of Soho keep many an hour.
      The Bohos of Soho,
      The Bohos of Soho,
      The Bohos of Soho,
      Have many lives,
           The Bohos of Soho are a good seed.

You and I,
In Soho,
For last orders.

———◆◆◆———

This poem was performed at Celine's Salon *Putting the Boho back in Soho* on 26th June 2019 at The Sanctum Hotel, London.

London-born Ashley grew up in Paris, Ibiza, Morocco and Lisbon. 'The Thames ebbs and flows on the tide and to her and my loved ones, eternal thanks.'

CATHY FLOWER

ICONS ARE EVERYWHERE

Invisible walks
Not wanting to be seen
Seldom visible escortations
Often alone
Radiant glow
She on the podium
That you cannot see
She's an artist
A writer
A painter
She's a pic taker
A singer
A dancer
She's a creator
She's a pianist
Eccentric
She burns
She cries
She smokes
She dies
She survives
Cos she
Is an Icon

We are canvases for
The clothing sculptors
The skin fashion designers
Who obscure and protect
Our frameworks
Innovate and style

Our scaffolds
Attaching new story
An extra personality
To our own
Icons they are
Some
Recognised

Sylvie lives above a fry
She repairs clothes
Has stitched for twenty two years
She banishes the odour
With essential oils in water
No fire fear
As she sews her brainchild
A pair of tight
Skin cuddling shorts
In cornflower blue velvet
For her fry man lover
He's downstairs shaking
Chips in a cage
Frying and flipping flavours
For the umpteenth time
Sweating for his wage
For his thirty eighth year
Sylvie is an Icon
Her fry man lover
Who gives his all
To serve well
Is an Icon too

The Tea Ladies
Less pour today
Poured continuously
Day after day
Many years have passed
Since their first pour for countless
Inserting smiles

Keeping the low at bay
They are Icons
In their own grace
Icons are everywhere
Creating
Inspiring
Humanising
Influencing
Losing and winning
They are household names
Or inconspicuous incandescing
Lights
That keeps the cogs
Of life
Spinning

———◼◆◆◆◼———

This poem was performed for Celine's Salon *Icons* on 3rd December 2018 at Gerry's Club, London.

Cathy Flower started writing and reading poetry in the late 1980s in Sydney where she was born. Pubs, art galleries, cafes and festivals were her platforms. In 2004 she moved to London hungry for the similar spread and happily found it with Celine's Salon. Her work has appeared in numerous anthologies, and she has written three poetry pamphlets, *There is a Tune* (W.C.H. Publishing 2015), *Blue Poetry* (Lalacuna Mayday Release 2013) and *Poetry is the Sight Within* (William Cornelius Harris 2010).

ANDREW BROWN

STUNNERS

Although I might have brushed past them in a gay bar or night club, I had never really met or talked to a transvestite or transsexual until around fifteen years ago when a London Friend introduced me to a louche semi-illegal nightclub in Limehouse called Stunners. It was run by a former antique and vintage car dealer originally christened Peter but now named Jayne. Over a few months I got to know her and her favourite clientele well and it was a revelation to me to being intimate with these brave transvestites, drag queens, and transsexuals and hear their often heart-breaking stories of ridicule and rejection from former friends and families, especially from those committed souls who were engaging in the full transition from male to female.

I painted Jayne's portrait several times, first in her home surprisingly modestly dressed in sweater, skirt and sandals, and later more typically in the club in a fabulous feather coat and hat like a coster queen or Edwardian dowager duchess.

She encouraged me to become a semi-official recorder of the club since photography was not allowed to protect the identity of the clientele who were prominent professionals and often happily married.

I set up a studio in the 'ladies' changing room and recorded the less timid clients in all their glory. Jayne likened our relationship to that of Toulouse Lautrec and La Goulie at the Parisian Follies or, like Francis Bacon and Muriel Belcher at The Colony Club in London's Soho.

It was a privileged insight into an exotic twilight world of tawdry glamour where I was completely accepted despite my personal lack of interest in dragging myself up. Indeed, when a new door person denied me entrance one night because I was night because I was neither in drag not fetish gear, Jayne swooped down like a great bird and pulled me in, declaiming 'tartan and tweed are Andrew's drag, dear.'

———————◆◆◆◆—————

This tale was performed at Celine's Salon *Putting the Boho back in Soho* on 26th June 2019 at The Sanctum Hotel, London.

Andrew Brown is a Scottish artist and art historian who founded the 369 Gallery in Edinburgh and has curated important exhibitions of Scottish art in the USA, China and Russia and brought major exhibitions of American, Russian and Ukrainian art to the Edinburgh Festival. He has exhibited widely in Europe and the USA and written several books on Scottish art including, *The Bigger Picture* which was made into an award-winning BBC television series.

PART SEVEN

Celine Hispiche
Tom Turner
Rebecca Anne Willis
Clayton Littlewood

CELINE HISPICHE

LIMEHOUSE SWAY

BETTY:
>In dear old Tidal Basin
>The dockers do fight
>The things you see amazing
>That's washed up in the night
>
>Clay pipes and broken china
>Old bones, a rusty shilling
>Sights that make you shudder
>And stories that are chilling
>
>The Thames a tub of black ink
>The flapping of the sails
>The smell of exotic spices
>Old bags of rusty nails
>
>Let's wander to the Dockland
>Yes, dear old Tiger Bay
>The clinking of the chains
>The bows of ships do sway
>
>>*chorus*
>>Sway, sway, sway
>>Let's dance to a Limehouse day
>>Sway, sway, sway
>>Let's all just drift away

FOUR DOCKERS:
>Wooah, wooah, wooah, wooah
>The work and the reminding
>That life is demanding
>So many mouths to feed
>Working every day
>In order to make some pay
>Is never very easy

Ten in a tiny room
Another on the way
Makes me hardly breathe

The missus be a nagging
'He's always out a supping'
What's a man to do?

> *chorus*
> Sway, sway, sway
> Let's dance to a drunken day
> Sway, sway, sway
> Me monies all gone away

COSTER LADIES:
> Let's wander down the causeway
> A sight for all to see
> Tiny little storefronts
> Selling Chinese remedies
>
> Papers lanterns are a swinging
> Mandarins with slippered feet
> The smell of oriental cooking
> Sweet and sour pork meat
>
> The costars sell their wares
> Fresh oysters or a herring
> You can even buy a canary
> A monkey if you're willing
> Ladies adorn hats
> With clouds of ostrich feathers
> Men in cheeky caps
> Wearing shoes of yellow leather

> *chorus*
> Sway, sway, sway
> Let's dance to a Limehouse day
> Sway, sway, sway
> Let's all just drift away

BETTY:

>And down crooked allies
>The fog lays so thick
>The barges snuggled together
>In the safety of Tidal Basin
>
>Strange conversations
>You hear now and then
>Dark ghostly shadows
>Coming out of the opium dens
>
>Ladies of the pavement
>Shiver in their shawls
>There ain't mistaking
>How dark the night does fall
>
>And then a friendly candle
>Whose flame flickers so
>Shooing us away
>It's time you children go

ALL:

>*chorus*
>Sway, sway, sway
>I tell ya what they say
>Sway, sway, sway
>It's time to call it a day
>Sway, sway, sway
>I don't care what they say
>
>Sway, sway, sway,
>Here's to a Limehouse
>Here's to a Limehouse
>Here's to a Limehouse day!

This song was performed at Celine's Salon *Music Hall* on 6th February 2017 at The Society Club, London.

TOM TURNER

ANECDOTE

Pictures painted on the TV
Always moving
Never ending
Electronic rivers constantly flowing through black lines on the wall
Sex, dreams, violence, teens, screams
You don't know where you stand no more
Why are there no more protest songs?

Radio is silent in the car
Plays only what you pay for
Music is free
Stealing me away, constantly played
Your nan's sitting in the front room, gramophone's outplayed
Scraping, sound, eager, spreads disease
You don't know where you stand no more
Why are there no more protest songs?

Video games
Violence stains
Mass consuming
Thought quenching time devouring facilities.
False lands flash through the darkness where it will clash at five am
Perverse, claim, minds of many
You don't know where you stand no more
Why are there no more protest songs?

Girls, girls, girls
24-hour service for the world
We all want more rights, while devils deal in price
Ten, eleven, twelve, for the hungry mouths that need to feed
Masturbating, shaming, disgraceful ways to fame, sounds force their
way into your ear, till all is clear
You don't know where you stand no more

Why are there no more protest songs?
Media
Telling you who you are
Fat, black, white, skinny, rich, tight, don't matter
You're all welcome if you fetch likes
Models, cars, clothes, money, stars, capitalism to make Marx blush
I don't know where I stand no more.

———————◼ ◆ ◆ ◼———————

This poem was performed at Celine's Salon *Memories and Special Moments* on 28th October 2019 at Gerry's Club, London.

Tom, 22, has been with Celine's Salon for a year. He says it's been a real pleasure, a great experience and it's a privilege to have his work in this anthology with so many talented people.

REBECCA ANNE WILLIS

A BRIEF ENCOUNTER

Beware, beware a brief encounter
Kicking to the ground.
One may see bliss
Where misery is found
And to your enchanting stranger
Forever you be bound.
Know this:
You skipped,
You danced
And laughed
Yet in love
Happiness is halved.
Beware the faces you know not
Before you find your own
Forgot
Then as the rose
Your sorrow grows
When that stranger
alone,
knows
Of all your hope
And all your pain
Of all the dreams you did not gain.
Yes,
Your stranger was standing still
Hiding, silently, lying.
So beware fresh spark
Travelling in dark;
You do not know the ending.

THE PANTHER'S PEN

I want a pen that slides and glides
So if a shadow falls upon my heart
It will write the wrongs
And tell the truth.
There is nothing
Yet there you are.
For you,
I am exhausted.
As pomegranate without seed
And heart that does not bleed,
Your hollow kiss is slithering
Within the child's wish.
See how the stars spread their smile across the sky,
What makes them delight?
That which makes them shine so bright?
In an instant I would go;
To find out,
To know
The purpose of dreams
And what does it mean
To be truly free?
A Panther crawling in my sheets
Has bitten me in sleep
Now I am awake
and the wound seeps.
I long for its mark
To press upon my face,
And trace itself along my limbs
With sickening
Wicked grace,
Singing songs of sorry woe
Giving me my seeds to sow.

L'ESPRIT TORTURÉ

See how the muses sing softly
Disturbing the sleeps
Of the soul that weeps.
Thrust into madness
You have been plunged
Into the evergreens
Of never changing seas
I fear you should not write
I fear you should not dream
It splits you down the centre;
The fragility of seams.
Now surely you are mad
As surely you are blessed
For both Angel and Demon,
Rest upon your chest.

———————◆◆◆———————

All three poems were performed at Celine's Salon *Bohemia* on 21st
February 2018 at the Med Café, London.

Rebecca Anne Willis is a London born and bred storyteller and poet
whose work aims to explore the trials of human emotion and identity.
Having trained in Design for Performance, Rebecca also enjoys putting on
a show and can often be found escaping the suburbs for the sunny sights
of Soho.

CLAYTON LITTLEWOOD

PICCADILLY, MY STOP

I step off the train, onto the escalator, up the stairs, until I'm above ground, on the Dilly Boy 'meat rack' of old, on the outskirts of Soho. I walk down Brewer Street, past the 'closing-down' Vin Mag, the NCP Car Park, my mood lifting as I enter the village, following in the footsteps of my heroes; Wilde, Crisp, Almond and Horsley.

I first came to Soho in the 80s, drawn by the Non-Stop Erotic Cabaret world of seedy films and sex clubs. I'd stand outside Madam JoJo's, gazing up at Marc's flat, or linger outside the Trident Studios on St Anne's Court (home to Bolan, Bowie and Freddie), hoping to catch a glimpse of my hero. Then at night, high on speed, I'd climb a rickety staircase on Wardour Street to The Pink Panther, mixing with rent boys and goth girls, East End crims and West End toffs, drag kings and scene queens, 'dancing, laughing, living, loving'. That was my Soho, so long ago.

From the dying embers of the sex industry (on Walker's Court) I cross the film world of Wardour Street, turning into the gay world of Old Compton Street. On my right, Cafe Espana. On my left, St Quentin's old haunt, The Black Cat (where he was beaten by 'the roughs'). The street's awash tonight, with tourists and hen nights, Hari Krishnas and socialites, a melting pot of London life, thrown together on one street, like a modern day Hogarth painting. I walk past the 2is (the birthplace of British rock and roll), a pack of bears outside Comptons (the new Coleherne clones), bowing my head in remembrance as I pass the Admiral Duncan, breathing in the rich aroma from the 125-year-old Algerian Coffee Shop, until I'm standing on the Dean Street crossroads. It was these magical few yards that Daniel Farson captured when chronicling Bacon's 'gilded gutter life', that 50s Love Is The Devil drunken period when he'd stagger from Gaston's bohemian The French House, to Muriel's 'concentration of camp' at The Colony, recovering over breakfast at number 50, Cafe Torino's, where a ten foot marionette once perched above the door, and where 'dark Italians and pale young artists and poets' would search half-heartedly for jobs. I have a connection to this building. This is where my partner and I once lived, in the damp rat-infested basement, just feet away from Elizabethan plague pits (and where I too would chronicle life on this street).

I turn into Dean Street, waving at Maggie, one of the madams from the 'walk up', heading for Meard Street, the little cobbled Georgian thoroughfare where the famous Soho clubs The Mandrake and The Gargoyle once stood; where Tallulah Bankhead danced, where Fred Astaire was entranced, where Farson took Josh Avery in the book Dog Days of Soho. The prettiest street in the village. Whenever I'm in Soho I make a point of coming here. I stand outside number seven, the house with the sign that reads,

'This is not a brothel. There are no prostitutes at this address,' and I remember. For it was here that Sebastian Horsely, the Soho dandy, once lived. I would ring his bell, the shutters would open on the first floor and he'd lean out, in a black silk negligee with a marabou feather–lined neck, his face coated in a fine white powder, his eyes caked in last night's mascara and he'd purr 'Hello Romeo, Juliet here. Welcome to Horsley Towers.' When he died his coffin was wrapped in blood-red tissue paper, draped in jewels and it was placed in a Victorian style horse-drawn hearse. And the hearse went all round the streets of Soho. It was as if Sebastian was saying a last goodbye to the village that he loved.

Now I'm back on Dean Street, looking toward The Golden Lion (a one time serial killer haunt). It was here I last saw Pam, the local homeless 'celebrity'. Wherever I was in Soho, Pam was here too. If I was walking past the Coach and Horses, Pam would step out of a doorway. If I was having a coffee outside Maison Bertaux, her radar would home in on me, dressed in her usual attire; camouflage trousers, donkey jacket, 'barn owl' NHS glasses, sporting a number one haircut. 'Gotta gold one for me?' she'd mumble. I'd hand her a coin. She'd squint at it, not looking impressed. 'It's all I've got, Pam.' Then she'd wrap her arms around me, snuffling into my jacket. 'Thank you ... Luv you!' And off she'd trundle, like something from

Beatrix Potter. Pam the Fag Lady. The hardest worker on Old Compton Street.

I turn left into Old Compton Street, and look, there's the woman with the striking eye makeup and the 'bum length' multi-coloured plaits. And over there, that's Michele, the aging trans woman, shuffling past, in a moth-eaten fur. Like an ancient Romanov in exile. This street may be predominately youth oriented, but the old return, often unnoticed, to remember, to reflect. They see a different Soho. The ghosts.

A minute later I'm at 'Fruit Corner', the proliferation of coffee shops on the corner of Frith Street, within sight of Kettners. It is said that Wilde and Lord Alfred Douglas entertained rent boys there. And a couple of decades before them, two other doomed lovers, Rimbaud and Verlaine, socialised in a public house on this street. And this is what I love about Soho—sitting in these coffee shops, by the window, writing in my notebook, watching the mayhem outside— I imagine the artists, the writers and the eccentrics that have flocked here over the centuries, attracted by the cosmopolitan feel, the lure of sex, and the hint of danger that lies within. You can't transport this vibe. It's in the brickwork. It's in their footsteps. The High Street chains may be moving in, but old Soho is still here if you care to look. There's nowhere like it in the world. And one day it will rise again. It always does.

———————◆◆◆———————

This story was performed at *Welcome to Celine's Salon* on 12th February 2016 at The Society Club, London

Clayton Littlewood was born and raised in England and now lives in Fort Lauderdale. A playwright and actor, he is the author of two books *Dirty White Boy: Tales of Soho* (Cleis Press 2008) which won the Gay Times Book of the Year award, and the sequel, *Goodbye to Soho* (DWB Press, 2012).

The play *Dirty White Boy: Tales of Soho* was performed by Clayton and the actor David Benson at the Trafalgar Studios in 2010 and returned two years later for an extended run.

CURTAIN

List of dates, themes & venues

12 Feb 2016—*Welcome to Celine's Salon*—The Society Club, London

2 March 2016—*Seven Deadly Sins*—The Society Club, London

5 April 2016- *Bad Behaviour*—The Society Club, London

4 May 2016- *Eccentricity*—The Society Club, London

1 June 2016—*Magic*—The Society Club, London

6 July 2016—*Horror*—The Society Club, London

7 September 2016—*Underwear*—The Society Club, London

3 October 2016 —*Wild West*—The Society Club, London

7 November 2016—*Gangsters*—The Society Club, London

5 December 2016—*Vinyl*— The Society Club, London

9 January 2017—*Forbidden Fruit*— The Society Club, London

6 February 2017—*Music Hall*— The Society Club, London

6 March 2017—*Unconventional*— The Society Club, London

14 June 2017—*Rebellion*— The Society Club, London

11 September 2017—*Berwick Street Market*—Med Café, London

13 October 2017—*The Art of Laughing*—The Barrel House, Totnes

15 Nov 2017—*In the footsteps of JMW Turner*—Med Café, London

21 February 2018—*Bohemia*— Med Café, London

28 March 2018—*The Supernatural*—Hummus Bros, London

25 April 2018 —*Arabian Nights*— Med Café, London

29 May 2018—*Punk*— Med Café, London

25 September 2018—*Gypsies*—Troy 22, London

3 December 2018—*Icons*—Gerry's Club, London

14 Jan 2019 —*Where the hell was I last night?*—Gerry's Club, London

6 February 2019 —*Nightclubbing*—The Sanctum Hotel, London

25 March 2019—*Brief Encounters*—Gerry's Club, London

13 May 2019—*Obsession*— Gerry's Club, London

26 June 2019—*Putting the Boho back in Soho*—The Sanctum Hotel

28 October 2019 —*Memories and Special Moments*— Gerry's Club

25 November 2019—*The Art of Persuasion*— Gerry's Club, London

12 December 2019—*Value*—Gerry's Club, London

27 January 2020 —*Zeitgeist*— Gerry's Club, London

27 February 2020—*Serendipity*— Gerry's Club, London

16 April 2020—*Zen*—Zoom

14 May 2020—*Left Field*—Zoom

11 June 2020—*Experimentation*—Zoom

26 June 2020—*On the Spot*—Zoom
3 March 2021—*Dreams*—YouTube
11 March 2021—*Dreams 2*—YouTube
17 March 2021—*Dreams 3*—YouTube
8 April 2021—*Is there life on Mars?*—YouTube
21 April 2021—*South Africa*—YouTube

Acknowledgements

I will always appreciate that beautiful summer day in 2015 when I walked into The Society Club on Silver Place. It was at this very bookshop that Babette gave me the opportunity and privilege to establish a night of performance and for Celine's Salon to be born. A huge and grateful thanks to Babette Kulik and Michael Selzer for giving us our start.

And so, the Salon grew, following The Society Club to Ingestre Place and then, after dear Violet gave me the heads up, to the Med Café on Berwick Street. Thanks so much for allowing me to use your bohemian basement, Ali Aksu, in loving memory of Violet.

As our events started bulging at the seams our next port of call and current residency is at the legendary Gerry's Club on Dean Street. Thank you to Michael Dillon, Alison Elderfield and Gentiana Vala for your support.

Since then, the Salon has been a travelling extravaganza too! Here's a big heartfelt thank you to all of the following:

Sarah Trigg and Richard Kidd at The Barrel House Totnes, Devon

The Troy Club, London

The Society Club, Cheshire Street, London

Mandy and Mark Fuller at The Sanctum Hotel, Soho, London

Carissa Warner and Vito Joes, Antigua

Adrian Meehan, Rachel Bird, Will Fitzpatrick at Soho Radio

Tony Shrimplin at Museum of Soho

Michelle Wright, Helena Gaunt and all at The Guildhall School of Music and Drama

Polly Bull for their help and support

Clancy Gebler Davies for production on our YouTube channel

Everyone who donated to Celine's Salon during lockdown to fund vital equipment for our online shows

Dave Crocker for his amazing art

My amazing and supportive husband/producer/polymath of the highest level, Garry Salter

Lucy Tertia George for believing in me and being an amazing inspiration

And finally, to all of our supporters, friends and performers without whom none of this could have happened!

Roll on Volume 2...